Praise for *Clay in the P*

"I thoroughly enjoyed *Clay in the Potter's Hands*. Diana Glyer's descriptions bring the process of creating pottery alive for us. She connects us to the men and women of Bible times for whom watching the potter at work would have been a daily experience. In so doing, she illustrates God's character and our discipleship in a unique and encouraging way. I recommend this book enthusiastically." **Cynthia Nicholson, National Women's Task Force Coordinator, Vineyard USA, Assistant Pastor, Vineyard Church of Evanston, Illinois**

"Most Christians have heard that God is the potter and we are the clay, but Diana Glyer, who has spent countless hours at the potter's wheel with her own hands saturated with clay, shows in this remarkable book that this saying is far more than a casual metaphor. God's fingerprints are all over us. As God hovers over his creation, centering us or shaping us or even restoring us from collapse, he may transform us in ways we never imagined. *Clay in the Potter's Hands* does a masterful job of revealing spiritual insights from an insider's perspective, as one potter considers the work of God the Master Artist. You will be challenged and inspired." **Joseph Bentz, Author of *A Son Comes Home*, *When God Takes Too Long*, and *God in Pursuit*, LaVerne, California**

"In her book, Diana Glyer provides vivid and captivating imagery that brings delight in being mere clay in the hands of our mighty Creator. Inspiring questions accompany each chapter, culminating in prayers that lead the reader to a humble awe and gratitude for being chosen and crafted into the image of God by the Potter's own hand." **Doug Greenman, Executive Pastor, Stanwood Foursquare Church, Stanwood, Washington**

"Before reading this book, I looked at the metaphor of the potter and the clay merely as a lesson of accepting the way God made me. This book has helped me see through the eyes of the potter and opened up a great many other lessons for me to meditate on. I felt so inspired by the lessons in the book." **Daniel Cothran, Missionary, Author of *Knowing the Difference: How to Recognize a Cult*, Tunghai University, Taiwan**

"This is a book to be savored. Devotional books like this one are rare; I don't remember the last time I read one which expresses the richness of Scripture with such simplicity, grace and practical application. My own "crack-pot" life experienced the shaping, restoring and encouraging hand of the Potter through reading this book. I highly recommend the experience." **Will Vaus, President of Will Vaus Ministries, Author of *Mere Theology* and *The Hidden Story of Narnia*, Monterey, Virginia**

"I find the general run of devotional books worse than useless; *Clay in the Potter's Hands* is a wonderful exception. A gifted writer who has thought long and hard about the Christian life and who has lived the biblical metaphor around which this work centers, she manages to be clear without being cloying, deep without being difficult, and spiritual without being sappy. She gives us everything the people who like devotional books are looking for without subjecting us to any of the things people who hate them are fleeing. This is a great achievement indeed." **Donald T. Williams, Pastor and Missionary, The Evangelical Free Church of America, Author of *Mere Humanity* and *Credo: Meditations on the Nicene Creed*, Professor of English, Toccoa Falls College, Toccoa, Georgia**

"I was very impressed with the imagery of the clay (me) going through the process of becoming something useful. I have given several books to friends of all ages. My pastor commented that his 11 year old daughter could read it to her 7 year old twin sisters as well as her 80+ year old grandmother. The book has traveled all over to friends and family. Thank you for writing it and allowing us to be part of your creativity." **Ruth E. Carlson, RN, Parish Nurse, Good Shepherd Evangelical Lutheran Church, Claremont, California**

"Never has the most careful Old Testament scholar explained Isaiah's image of the potter and the clay (Is. 45:9) better than Diana Glyer in *Clay in the Potter's Hands*. Never again will I look at a clay pot in the same ordinary way. Neither will you. Read it slowly, devotionally, one chapter a day. Think on each chapter, pray over it, and find yourself molded, changed, enlightened, and encouraged." **Joel Heck, Professor of Theology, Concordia University Texas**

"Diana Glyer teaches like Jesus. This poetic parable of the pots got to my head *and* to my heart." **Greg Anderson, Senior Pastor, Union Church, Hong Kong**

"This is a really good book! It manages to combine depth and simplicity which is rare, but I think it is the way it treats our experience of pain and broken-ness which really sets it apart. The chapters on Returning, Repairing and Redeeming were especially moving and significant for me. This book is going to be so helpful to so many people!" **Malcolm Guite, Priest, Poet, Chaplain at Girton College, University of Cambridge, Author of** *Faith, Hope, and Poetry,* **Cambridge, England**

"*Clay in the Potter's Hands* is a strong, extended metaphor that takes what is already a good analogy and makes it much more profound. When we hear the Apostle Paul say that we are like clay to God the Potter, we hardly realize that each stage of the process of shaping the artisan's work serves as a unique analogue to something that God does in the process of shaping us. In our modern world of prefab housewares, that analogy could well have been lost, had not Glyer recaptured it for us." **James W. Miller, Senior Pastor, Glenkirk Presbyterian Church, Author of** *God Scent: A Devotional*

"I used Diana Glyer's *Clay in the Potter's Hands* for my Ceramics classes. The students loved identifying with well known Biblical stories as they worked at mastering the potter's wheel." **Susan Ney, Artist and Professor, Azusa Pacific University, Azusa, California**

"Rarely does one encounter a writer who seizes a powerful metaphor, digs deeply into its heart, and allows it to shape and inform not only her prose but her life. In *Clay in the Potter's Hands*, Diana Glyer has done just that. Here, we gently move from observer to participant and from casual knowledge to redeeming wisdom. Each step of this shaping process is filled with meaning and each meditative moment is touched with the eternal hand of the Master Potter. Diana Glyer invites her readers into the *real* potter's studio." **Scott B. Key, Professor of Philosophy, California Baptist University, Riverside, California**

"Fascinating! As a potter, I could identify with the different stages of creating with clay, and as a Christian, I appreciated how this book ties each step into how God works in our lives. From the beginning to the end—God is able to use us—if we are yielded and still. Thank you for this insight and testimony of faith which has enriched my life." **Pat Ballard, Artist, Westchester, California**

"I've read dozens of devotional books. Ok, well, I've *started* dozens of them, but with very few exceptions they usually leave me uninspired. But Diana Glyer has managed the nearly impossible: to sound the deep places of the heart with healing, humor, wisdom and grace. The way she does it—suggesting rather than saying, leaving all kinds of room for the reader—makes this book uniquely effective in all of the devotional reading I have ever done. I read one chapter a day, and without fail always felt the Great Physician using Diana's care-filled, honest humility and spare, rich prose to open up my heart for that divine surgery that cuts even as it cleanses. I do not exaggerate to say that I left tears of joy, release, refreshment and grace on every single page. It's that good. It's better—it's superb and so full of grace and truth that it has become a profound treasure. *Clay in the Potter's Hands* moved me to the depths of my soul." **Andrew Lazo, Speaker, Co-editor of *Mere Christians: Inspiring Stories of Encounters with C. S. Lewis*, Teacher, St. Thomas High School, Houston, Texas**

"There is only so much the average reader can take away from the verses in Jeremiah about the potter and the clay without a little help. With Diana Glyer's inspirational book as my guide, I've been able to understand the deeper meaning of what scripture says regarding the Christian walk. I have felt inspired, encouraged, and definitely stretched. I especially enjoyed the discussion questions, as they require me to put into practice what I've just read. The prayers that end each section are both inspiring and, sometimes, a bit unnerving as I found myself reading a prayer that could have come straight from my own heart." **Richard McCoy, Special Education Teacher and Motivational Speaker, Laquey, Missouri**

"There is a tremendous need in each person's life to know God's reality, to feel His presence, to experience His guidance and love. Read *Clay in the Potter's Hands*. Like it did for me, it will open your eyes to the way God shapes us and loves us in a life-changing way. I cannot recommend a book on spiritual formation more highly to you—and your whole family!" **John Trent, Founder and President of StrongFamilies.com and The Center for StrongFamilies, Phoenix, Arizona, Author of *The Language of Love, The Gift of Honor, Heart Shift, The Two-Degree Difference*, and *The Blessing***

"In one hundred pages, Diana Glyer offers her readers fifteen marvelous chapters for reflection and more. You can "feel" her love of pottery and join her as she tells the story of creating something beautiful. Each chapter of *Clay in the Potter's Hands* offers the reader an opportunity to accompany the potter at work. The author gently and easily moves from the potter's wheel to texts from the Bible that offer examples of each stage of development of the artist's work. These are accompanied by marvelous insights and questions for the reader to consider; then each chapter concludes with a prayer that brings the entire segment together quite nicely.

As a Jesuit, I found this work very appealing. St. Ignatius suggested the use of imagination for contemplative prayer. The Scripture texts that Glyer has chosen, together with the fascinating story of making and repairing pottery, would alone be helpful toward contemplative prayer. However, she has gone further. Each chapter is a movement from the wheel where clay is worked to a "wheel" where a healthy spiritual life is formed. The entire book could be read rather quickly, but I suggest that the reader savor each chapter as a daily prayer. There will be no disappointments." **Father John Chandler, S.J., Honolulu, Hawaii**

Clay in the Potter's Hands

Clay in the Potter's Hands

LENT 2015

Diana Pavlac Glyer

DIANA PAVLAC GLYER

Photographs by Adam Bradley

Lindale & Assoc.
A Division of TreeHouseStudios

CLAY IN THE POTTER'S HANDS

Copyright © 2011 by Lindale & Associates
a Division of TreeHouseStudios

Photographs © 2011 Adam Bradley

Cover and Design by The Seven-Seventy Design Group
Photo of the author (color) by Tira J Photography

Scripture taken from THE HOLY BIBLE, NEW INTERNATIONAL VERSION.
Copyright © 1973, 1978, 1984 by the International Bible Society.

Publisher's Cataloging-in-Publication Data

    Glyer, Diana.
       Clay in the potter's hands / Diana Pavlac Glyer ;
    photographs by Adam Bradley.
       p. cm.
       ISBN-13: 978-0-578-04501-6
       ISBN-10: 0-578-04501-X

       1. Spiritual formation. 2. Christian life.
    I. Title.

BV4501.3.G59 2010   248.4
                  QBI10-600005

First Edition 2011
Printed in the United States of America

This book is dedicated to Dr. Laura K. Simmons:

Tuo esset bene dictum.

May this book be a good word
as you embrace the new adventure that Christ
is making of your life day by day.

Acknowledgements

I owe a great debt of thanks to many people who have encouraged and supported me, not only in this project but in the ongoing process of recognizing and cooperating with the hand of God in my daily life. In writing this book, I would like to acknowledge the faithful collaboration of these dear friends:

...the Niños, creative artists who have persevered in prayer;

...the United Methodist Annual Conference on Prayer and Healing, coordinated under the leadership of Dave Walker, for providing time and encouragement for the workshops that this book is based upon;

...Susan Ney, who flung open the door of the APU ceramics studio and changed my life forever;

...Lynn Maudlin, who came to the rescue;

...Chase Pielak, who threw cylinders and loaded that heavy wheel into my car weekend after weekend, without complaint;

...Jane Ellen Louise Beal, who convinced me that it was possible;

...Andrew Lazo, a wellspring of so much that is good in my life;

...Adam Bradley, my nephew and my friend (I love you more);

...Linda Sherman Spitser, the best editor I have ever, ever, ever worked with;

...Kayla Winiarz Karesh, Alene Campbell, Kim Bangs, James Watkins, Nick Harrison, and Dan McCracken, who commented on rough drafts and made this a much better book;

...and always, my dear Michael, because every book I write is built upon the foundation of kindness and faith that you bring to each day of our life together.

Contents

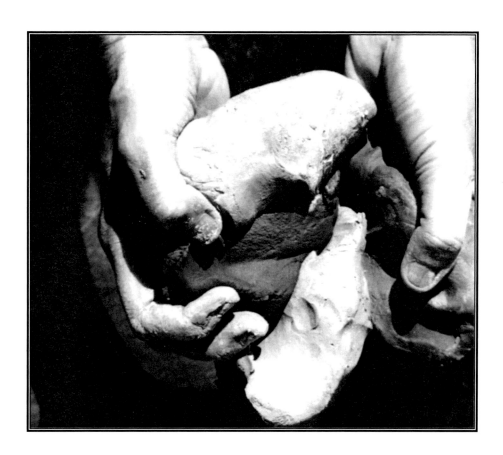

Introduction

I got into ceramics by accident—at least it seemed so at the time. As a child, I was a big fan of a Disney movie called *The Three Lives of Thomasina*. In it, a cat named Thomasina becomes a bridge of understanding between a father and his daughter. One of the characters in the film is Laurie, a weaver. As I watched her pull and set the threads in line after line of color and pattern, as I listened to the sound of those large wooden shuttles rocking back and forth, I discovered that weaving is a creative act that brings together the very best of color and pattern and music and dance. I was enchanted by it. Years later, when I was a senior in high school, my counselor told me that I needed to sign up for an elective art class, and I jumped at the chance—I registered for Weaving 101.

When my schedule arrived, I noticed the mistake right away. Instead of being in Weaving 101, I was registered for Ceramics 101. Ceramics? I wasn't even sure what ceramics was. Pouting and resentful, I decided to attend the class just once, then meet with my counselor at the end of the day and explain that I couldn't *possibly* stay in that class. And then I'd rearrange things so that I'd get what I wanted in the first place.

But something happened in my heart when I walked into that ceramics studio. I watched the potter spin a small lump of clay on the potter's wheel then pull it tall into a cylinder then shape it into a pot—in minutes a magic transformation had taken place. The simple lump of clay was changed forever into something of worth and beauty. I was changed, too. I wanted to be a potter.

I never did get into that weaving class, but I have been working on the potter's wheel ever since. Being an artist is one of the deepest and highest things I do. Deepest because it so completely satisfies my heart. Highest because it lifts me, wordlessly, effortlessly, happily, into communion with my Creator.

In the Bible, it says that God is like a potter, and that we are like clay. This beautiful image has special meaning for me, and I marvel at it every time I go to the ceramics studio, sit at the wheel, and begin my work. It seems to me that the more we know about clay, kilns, wheels, grog, firing, glazing, wedging, and the like, the more this spiritual picture becomes vivid and useful in our daily lives.

In this little book, I will share some of the rich meaning of this picture—God is the potter, we are the clay. And I will encourage you to reflect, to think and pray and discuss with others the significance of this transforming image in your own life.

Diana Pavlac Glyer

1 Creating

God tells us that he is like a potter working with clay.

Throughout the Bible, God uses word pictures to tell us what he is like. God is like a loving shepherd. A good neighbor. A strong tower. Of all the pictures that God offers, one of the earliest and most persistent is this: God is like a potter and we are like clay.

It all starts in the beginning, with the creation story in the book of Genesis. God speaks, and all of creation explodes into existence: Let there be light! Let there be land! Let there be water, plants, and living things! The scene is enormous, the work is glorious, the voice of the Lord is majestic, and the action is on the largest possible scale.

That is the glory of Genesis chapter one. But turn the page, and everything is changed. The theme that just a moment before was as big as the universe is suddenly small and quiet and very, very personal. You can almost hear a hush as God moves across the fresh, green world and begins a new work of creation: "The Lord God formed the man from the dust of the ground and breathed into his nostrils the breath of life" (Genesis 2:7).

The Lord God formed the man. And look at how he did it. The word that is translated "formed" comes from the Hebrew word *yatsar*, and *yatsar* refers to forming, stretching, squeezing, pressing, and molding something into a specific shape.

That word, *yatsar*, is quite literally the creative action of a potter working with clay—in fact, the very same word is used in Jeremiah 18 and 19, where the prophet goes to the house of the potter and watches as the clay is centered, opened, stretched, and shaped on the potter's wheel.

Throughout scripture, there are many different images of God, an outpouring of images that help us understand what God is like. Here, in the Genesis account, in the beginning, God has chosen the image of the potter and the clay, and he repeats that image many times. For example, in Jeremiah 18:6, it says we are like clay in the hands of a potter. In Isaiah 45:9, we are called clay, and in Romans 9:21, we are called lumps of clay. In Isaiah 29:16, 2 Corinthians 4:7 and 2 Timothy 2:20, we are called clay pots or jars of clay or earthen vessels. In Isaiah 64:8b, it says, "We are the clay, you are the potter; we are all the work of your hand."

What attributes of potters and clay *in particular* help us understand why God would describe his work in just this way?

The potter stoops low over the pot to shape it.

In order to work at the potter's wheel, the potter must stoop low, sit down, and settle in. The potter's wheel is surrounded, almost embraced, by the potter's body. In Genesis 1:2, we read that the Holy Spirit hovers over the face of the waters. In creation, God steps down. Comes near. Bends low. Hovers close.

This is true of creation; it is also true of incarnation. Jesus came down from heaven, took flesh, and dwelt among us. Jesus reached out and touched lepers, hugged sinners, held children. The same God who flung stars across the skies wrapped a towel around himself, knelt down, and washed the feet of his disciples.

The potter must stoop low over the pot to shape it; pottery making depicts a creator who stoops low and draws very near.

Clay gets all over the potter as the potter works with clay.

Some art forms allow for the artist to work at a polite distance. A sculptor might stand with hammer and chisel, chipping away at a block of marble. A painter holds brushes to apply paint to canvas. But when I work with clay, it soaks into my hands, slips under my fingernails, splatters on my clothes, gets caught in my hair. I was sitting at a formal luncheon recently and turned to introduce myself to a student sitting at our table. She grinned as she said to me, "I hardly recognize you now, but we have met before. I visited your art class a few months ago. The last time I saw you, Professor, you were covered with clay!"

It's true: as I reach out to touch the clay, it gets all over me. And throughout my day, it seems that I am always finding smudges of clay here and there. No matter how long I spend at the sink, cleaning up, getting ready to deliver a lecture on Shakespeare or go out on a dinner date with my husband, inevitably I seem to discover (too late!) that I have somehow missed a spot, and the clay still marks my hands. I can't escape it.

When I've been sitting at the wheel for a while, the water saturates my hands and the wet, slippery clay works itself into the folds of skin at my knuckles, and tucks itself into the spaces between my fingers. I can't get away from it.

Even more—eventually, as my hands have been immersed in art-making for a while, tiny, tiny bits of clay work themselves into the very pores of my skin. And stay there. I can't avoid it.

In Isaiah 49:15b-16, the Lord says, "I will not forget you! See, I have engraved you on the palms of my hands." In a similar way, the clay becomes quite literally etched into the potter's skin.

Clay gets all over the potter as the potter works with the clay; pottery making illustrates God's constancy and intimacy.

The soft, responsive nature of clay means that fingerprints are easily left in the surface of the vessel.

You can go to a museum and see clay vessels that are thousands of years old. Despite the passage of time, they still bear the marks of the potter who made them. It's not just that these clay vessels reflect the creative talent of the potter's personality. It's something more: there are actual marks pressed into the clay. Think of it—although those human fingers turned to dust ages ago, the clear imprint of those fingerprints remains.

All artwork bears the mark and reveals the nature of the artist. But clay is very responsive, and compared to other art forms, clay shows forth those literal fingerprints more clearly. The Christian who responds to God's call bears the mark of the Redeemer just as the pot that has been sought, prepared, shaped, and fired bears the mark of the one who made it.

Clay responds sensitively and permanently to the touch of the potter; pottery making represents God's certain touch on our lives.

Questions for Reflection and Discussion:

God is a creator, an artist, a maker. Reflect on a time that you have made things—anything, from rebuilding a carburetor to writing a song to coloring with crayons. What steps did you take to complete the work? What feelings did you have as you progressed from step to step? Did you sense that your creativity was a divine gift, a reflection of the creative nature of God? In what ways?

List several times that you have clearly seen the fingerprints of God in the circumstances of your life. Then take time to thank God for it!

Prayer:

You who are the King of all creation have stooped low to care for me. You who oversee all galaxies have become intimately involved in everything that concerns me. You who are the mighty one still bear the marks of your creation on your hands. Open my eyes, God, to see you more clearly in this season of my life than I ever have before. I wait expectantly for fresh insight into who you are, and who I am in you. Amen.

2
Searching

The potter actively seeks the clay and rejoices when it is found.

It is still early in the morning as the potter finishes the last bits of breakfast. He clears the dishes, picks up an old, gnarled walking stick, and heads out through the woods behind his home. He walks along the creek bank, and then climbs up the narrow path that leads into the surrounding hills. He is looking for clay.

Clay is formed in the earth when rain falls on rocks, dissolving minerals, oxides, and organic materials. As these are washed along, they blend together and are deposited along the river bank, or they settle at the bottom of a shallow lake or stream. Silt and dirt accumulate on top of it, plants take root, and there it remains. Hidden.

Hidden until the potter goes looking for it. Hiking far from home, climbing into the hills, searching through forgotten pathways, digging through layers of debris.

When a potter searches for clay, it is like a miner who tunnels through the earth to find a deposit of gold or copper, silver or jewels (Proverbs 2:4). It is like a merchant who looks for fine pearls (Matthew 13:45-46). Or a fisherman who searches the sea for a catch of fish (Matthew 13:47-49). Or a woman who carefully seeks a lost coin (Luke 15:8-10). Or a father who looks longingly day after day for his son who is lost (Luke 15:11-31).

Or a shepherd who goes after that one little lamb: "Suppose one of you has a hundred sheep and loses one of them. Does he not leave the ninety-nine in the open country and go after the lost sheep until he finds it? And when he finds it, he joyfully puts it on his shoulders and goes home" (Luke 15:4-6a).

In Ezekiel 34:15-16, God shows us more of his shepherd heart: "I myself will tend my sheep," says the Lord. "I will search for the lost and bring back the strays. I will bind up the injured and strengthen the weak." God loves us, values us, eagerly seeks for us, and rejoices over us when we are found.

The good shepherd knows his sheep—each is unique in many ways. Clay is like that, too. Depending on the particular mix of minerals and other raw materials, each kind of clay takes on a unique quality and character. The texture will vary from coarse and gritty to silky and smooth. It may be porous or dense, sticky or crumbly, soft or solid. Even the color differs from clay to clay, ranging from bright whites to pale ivories to rich reds to chocolate browns to midnight blacks.

The specific qualities of the clay, its porosity, plasticity, appearance, firing temperature, all will vary according to the qualities that are inherent in that particular clay. These qualities are not added on later—they are built into the very composition of the clay's nature. The type of clay with its inherent nature is called the *clay body*.

A good potter recognizes the unique and beautiful qualities of each type of clay. The amount of pressure that the clay can tolerate, the amount of heat that it needs to reach its potential—these factors and more will vary from clay to clay, and the good potter understands the differences.

Chances are you know a family where the kids are very different from one another. One child is placid, another fussy. One wakes at a whisper, the other sleeps through a thunderstorm. One is sunny and cheerful; another thoughtful, moody. One is impatient, restless, ready for any new thing. Another is cautious, resistant to change.

My family is like that. When I was a child, I was a typical first born in many ways: Sensitive. Obedient. I was like porcelain. When I did something wrong, all my mom had to do was to give me "that look" and say my full name. I knew I was in trouble. I would dissolve into tears, devastated.

My sister, on the other hand, is made of sterner stuff. She is, in many ways, a typical second born: Resilient. Collected. She is like earthenware. When she did something wrong, mom could pull out all the stops—scolding, swatting, threatening, punishing. My sister knew she was in trouble. But she would just look my mom in the eye and shrug, unfazed.

Wise parents know how to adapt to the particular temperament of each child; in order to be fair, they must handle each individual a little differently. Wise teachers know how to adjust the requirements of a class to the interests and abilities of their students. Wise potters know how to adapt to the particular temperament of the clay. And God in all his wisdom knows what is best. He has searched me and known me and called me by name.

Questions for Reflection and Discussion:

God has been seeking you all of your life. If you have responded to his call and been found by him, take time now to thank him for the way he has made you his own. If you have never responded, take time now to consider what it might mean for you, a wandering lamb, to be found and taken home to his fold. Then find someone who can tell you more about the Good Shepherd who loves you.

Each type of clay has unique qualities; each of us is unique in personality, abilities, and gifts. Spend some time journaling about the ways in which you are a unique lump of clay. Then ask God to show you how these unique qualities are strengths that he can use.

Prayer:

God, in your goodness, keep seeking after me, bringing me home, drawing me to your side. Thank you that you see in me something of infinite worth. I want to be used by you to do something of great importance. Show me the way to become available so that your miraculous hand can do mighty things on earth through me. Amen.

3 Preparing

The potter pulls the clay out of the earth and cleans and prepares it.

By the time the potter finds the clay and digs it out of the ground, it has been pressed into the earth for quite a while. As a result, certain impurities are embedded in it. There are small rocks, twigs, bits of leaf and bone, all the result of having been pressed against the world. Many of these things are very small and don't seem to be particularly significant. The clay looks great: clean and smooth and pure. But if these foreign objects are not removed, there will be very serious consequences in the life of the pot.

A little sliver of wood, a tiny stone, a pocket of air, or seed, sand, root, or twig. It is possible that such things will stay hidden for a long, long time. But in the firing process, in the heat of the kiln, nothing can stay hidden for long. It will react in the heat. The pot will explode, sometimes collapsing into a heap of rubble, sometimes flying apart with so much force that sharp bits of clay are embedded into the sides of the pottery around it.

You see, pots are shaped individually, one by one on the potter's wheel, but they go through the firing process together. Hidden debris becomes evident in the testing by fire, and the result can be an entire batch of pots all scarred and ruined by the one small, personal, private flaw.

I know of families that relate to one another very well most of the time. But then, suddenly, tough times come. A job is lost. A child becomes ill. Finances become tight. And some small issue—a sin that was hidden, a situation that was ignored, a personal habit that was carefully managed in the good times—becomes a kind of time bomb. And individuals and families are blown apart.

I have heard that the main reason Christian missionaries leave the mission field is that they have conflicts with other missionaries. In the heat of moving away from what is familiar, making the necessary adaptations to a new culture, and trying to establish a new work, character flaws and hidden sins begin to do damage.

Even good times can become the testing ground for character flaws and unfinished business. How many times has something as exciting as a family vacation become the opportunity for God to turn up the heat and see what is really in our hearts?

Flaws and impurities will come to light in the fire of testing, but, in general, most of them are discovered and dealt with earlier, before the pot is placed in the kiln. This is for the good of the pot, and for the safety of the other pots around it. But it is also to protect the potter. Stones, sticks and other small items become dangerous in the shaping process. This debris, the clutter of these impurities, has to be dealt with or it can scratch or even puncture the potter's hands.

Because this is such a serious matter, the wise potter takes extra care at this stage of the process. The clay is cleaned of every kind of impurity. It is carefully examined, and stones, sticks and other materials are carefully removed. It might even be put through a screen in order to eliminate even the smallest thing that might be harmful.

I had a recent experience that helped to remind me of what it means for even the smallest things in our lives to be carefully dealt with. I was on campus at the university where I teach, and one of my students came to my office and asked if she could talk with me. Her blue eyes quickly filled with tears as we sat down, and she blurted out, "I'm so ashamed of what I've done! I haven't been able to sleep or anything. I saw you today and my heart started beating so fast it scared me."

I didn't have any idea what she meant—I couldn't imagine what could be causing such distress. She lowered her eyes, "I cheated on my last quiz. I added an extra answer right after we graded them in class, right before we turned them in. It was only two extra points. It was such a small thing. But I don't care anymore what happens about my grade. I just need to let you know that I was wrong, and I'm so sorry."

I hugged her tight. Cheating on a daily quiz was a small thing.

Coming to confess it was a big thing. I thanked her for her courage, and told her that I would deduct those two points and correct her grade.

Then I thanked her again and told her that her desire to maintain absolute integrity filled me with admiration. "You are a model of what it is like to walk in Christ, sensitive to his word, quick to obey the prompting of his Spirit. That gift of a sensitive soul is one of the most important gifts God could give you. Don't ever let anything compromise that strong desire to make things right."

I know something about the damage that even small things can cause.

Questions for Reflection and Discussion:

Are there things in your life, large or small, that God wants to remove from your life because they hurt his heart and injure other people?

Are there people you need to talk to in order to settle a matter that has caused stress, tension, shame, or uneasiness?

Prayer:

O God, there are things in my life that I thought were private issues or insignificant matters. But now I see that they really are dangerous. They hurt me, hurt you, hurt others. I have not dealt with them the way I should. I confess that I've been wrong. Trusting in your goodness, I give you full permission to remove _____ from my life. I surrender it to you, knowing that even small things will pierce your hands. I surrender it to you, convinced that even small things will hurt my sisters and my brothers. Remove the rocks, sticks, stones, and bubbles in my soul, and fill the empty places with healing balm and the presence of your Holy Spirit, in Jesus' name. Let this be my prayer day by day. Amen.

4
Committing

The clay is wedged and then firmly attached to the potter's wheel.

After the clay is completely cleaned, it is wedged, a process that looks a lot like kneading dough. It is an important step, requiring patient attention from the potter. It involves a satisfying rhythm of pressing, turning, pressing, turning.

Wedging brings air bubbles and any remaining impurities to the surface so that they can be easily removed.

Wedging also builds consistent texture in all parts of the clay. The texture of the clay needs to be the same through and through. Any parts that are stiff or mushy are evened out. Moisture is distributed evenly throughout the clay (and isn't it interesting that water, moisture, is used throughout the Bible as a symbol of the Holy Spirit!).

There is one more thing that wedging does: it brings the clay particles into alignment. If you could look under a microscope, you would see that the clay is made up of flat plates, sort of like dinner plates. In raw clay, these plates are facing all different directions— horizontal, vertical, and at every possible angle. Wedging causes thesc flat plates to come into alignment, facing together in the same direction, and this unity gives the clay much greater strength.

I like to think of it as clay brought into harmony, all parts of it balanced and at peace. In James 1:7, it says that when we are double-minded, we are unstable in all our ways. With great care and patience, the potter wedges the clay so that all of the clay particles are in accord, and so that every part of that clean ball of clay is stable and strong.

These quiet, rhythmic, repeated motions bring the clay to a state of complete consistency. When it is ready, the potter lifts the wedged clay and gently pats it into an oval shape. Then, with a motion that is swift and deliberate, the potter holds the clay aloft and *smacks* it against the flat, round surface of the potter's wheel. Commitment. Why such a sudden, strong, almost violent action? Because the clay has to be fully and completely attached to the potter's wheel in order for the potter to do anything more with it.

Moments of commitment are all around us: they are clear, measurable, memorable, powerful. A marriage ceremony. A job contract. A college application. A license to practice medicine or law or pastoral ministry. The vows that lead to the monastic life. Throughout our lives, we are brought to precise and specific moments of decision, moments that are often accompanied by a ceremony or a ritual.

Each one represents a swift and deliberate point of commitment. I remember when our godsons were dedicated to God, and, in a beautiful ceremony, we made a vow to pray for them, care for them, and invest our time and energy and resources into their little lives. They were tiny, pink, and perfect, cooing in their blue blankets, sweet and adorable and uncomplicated. To make that commitment was easy.

Now we are faced with a commitment to keep. Those precious godsons have grown. They are loud and lively, bursting with energy and full of life. They live over an hour away, and our schedules, and theirs, are often stuffed full. Keeping up with them and blessing and caring for them on an ongoing basis is complicated. Commitment was quick and easy. But persistence is long and hard.

Just as there are things that can compromise the strength of our personal commitments, so there are things that compromise the tight commitment that keeps the clay firmly attached to the wheel. When the potter first begins to work on the wheel, a little bit of water may slip under the clay. Or, in the process of attaching the clay, a tiny bit of air might get trapped underneath. These can damage the seal that holds the clay tight to the spinning potter's wheel. If this happens, then as soon as potter starts to apply a little pressure, the clay will slide sideways and fly off.

In order for the potter to work, nothing can be spinning out of control, slopping over the sides, slipping to the floor, running for the door. The only way for the potter to work on the clay is for the clay to be firmly attached to the wheel. And then for it to *stay* firmly attached to the wheel.

I think of a doctoral student working to prepare for comprehensive exams. Day after day, week after week. And sometimes she wonders if it's worth it.

I think of a scientist, patiently going to the lab day after day, working on research. Intricate, repeated, painstaking steps.

A mother working with a child who's unruly.

A teacher working with a student who's dyslexic.

An athlete training for a contest that is months, even years, away.

A physical therapist working with a patient, struggling together to restore movement to an injured hand.

So often in our lives, it isn't the big challenges that defeat us. It's the small, daily challenges that spring forth from a specific commitment to a person, a project, a job, a contract, a mission, a way of life, and then after time become little more than a chore, a grind.

It isn't the two-week vacation backpacking in the mountain heights; it's walking the daily path from home to work step by step by step by step by step.

It isn't wrestling a mountain lion. It's being bitten to death by ducks.

Following God means cultivating faithfulness. He tells us we shouldn't put our hands to the plow and then look back—the work gets done when there is commitment and single-minded, persistent devotion (Luke 9:62).

God has taken the initiative: like a potter who seeks after the clay, God has sought us, drawn us to himself, cleaned us up, and prepared us. There comes a time for us to make a specific and whole-hearted response. We commit our lives to Christ.

And having made that commitment, we persevere. We resist the temptation to give up. We stick with it, even when it becomes inconvenient, annoying, uncomfortable, or dangerous to do so.

Questions for Reflection and Discussion:

Has God convinced you of any area of your life that is not going well because you haven't made a decisive commitment? If so, take time to make that commitment sure.

Think about the long-term projects that you are in the midst of. List them. Then ask for God's help to strengthen your resolve and help you finish well.

Prayer:

Forgive me, Gracious Heavenly Father, for the times I have broken my commitments because the situation just got too hard. Show me if I need to take steps to repair any damage I have caused. And now, rekindle hope in my heart to face the challenges that are before me this day. Give me the strength and courage to persevere in those things that you have called me to do. And when I come to the end of my life, let me say with the Apostle Paul, "I have fought the good fight, I have finished the race, I have kept the faith" (2 Timothy 4:7). Then let me run the race, this day, with cheerful endurance. Amen.

5
Centering

The potter spins the potter's wheel, applies water, and centers the clay.

When I am working with students, they are always looking for shortcuts. But mastering a creative art takes time, and the beginning steps may be tedious and frustrating: the painter stretches canvas, the pianist practices scales, the dancer repeats a step or a turn, the photographer memorizes aperture tables. The one part in the process that causes my students the most frustration is the time it takes to center the clay. It's not that hard. It just takes a really long time.

Once the clay is attached to the wheel, the potter spins it. Most potters use electric wheels. The speed of the wheel is controlled by a pedal that looks just like the gas pedal in your car. As the pedal is pressed, the wheel spins faster or slower, depending on the kind of work the potter is doing. Some potters prefer kick wheels or treadle wheels, non-electric wheels that are powered and controlled by the movements of the potter's feet.

The process of making a pot on the potter's wheel is called *throwing*. It is a funny term, but it has a long history in our language. The idea of throwing, or a throw, is the idea of shaping something as it turns. It is the turning or spinning of the wheel, the centrifugal force, that the potter uses to shape a lump of clay into a cup, vase, or bowl.

But first the clay must be centered; that is to say, every part and every aspect of it must be lined up with the very heart of the wheel.

When the lump of clay first starts to spin, it is obviously off-center—it is oddly shaped, it wobbles to and fro, it follows its own path, it is headed in many directions all at the same time.

The potter takes a little water to moisten his or her hands, then presses them against the spinning clay, pushing the clay closer to the *wheel head,* smoothing uneven places, pressing bumpy edges. The potter uses just enough pressure to center all parts of the clay. If the clay is stiff or the lump is large, it may take quite a bit of pressure to make the clay obey.

It may also take a surprisingly long time. And when you are watching a potter work on this step, it looks like nothing much is happening. I know that clay can't speak, but I've often thought that if it could, it would definitely express impatience at this point in the process: *"Aren't we done yet? Can't we move on? Isn't this right yet? Can't we do something different now? Haven't we been doing this long enough? Didn't you just do that a minute ago? Are you sure we're getting anywhere?"*

Centering takes time. But it is absolutely critical that every aspect of the clay is lined up. One small wobble now will spell disaster later—it won't affect the shape of things for the moment, but it will bump the whole pot out of kilter if it is not lined up right now. All of the clay must be centered. Like a machine with no added parts. Like a runner with no wasted motions. Like a symphony with no unnecessary notes. Like a gymnast perfectly controlled down to the tips of her fingers and her toes.

This idea of being centered is a powerful one for me, for my life is very busy, and I confess that unless I am very, very careful, I go running off in all directions. I have yet to master what it means to live in the absolute center, in the Great Shalom, in the peace of God. The Hebrew word *Shalom* is a powerful word meaning absolute tranquility. It means doing things with natural ease, not with frantic force or fearful striving. It means responding to life's challenges with a sense of creativity and optimism and resilience. It is a sense in my body and soul of well-being, safety, harmony, vibrant health. To be at ease, inside and out. Shalom. Aligned.

While Shalom includes all of this, the root of the word is wholeness. When Jesus instructs us to be perfect, he means we are to be whole, mature, grown-up, living in the fullness of all that God intends for us. Shalom. Complete.

When I think about the rich meaning of the word Shalom, I am tempted to get overwhelmed all over again. All of this seems more than I can bear, and it threatens to set me to more fretting and striving. Isn't it ironic: remind me of the gift of Shalom, and I am tempted to write "get some Shalom" on my to-do list right after "do the laundry" and "buy eggs and milk."

It helps when I remember the powerful promise of Philippians 1:6a: "He who began a good work in you will carry it on to completion." God began it. God will complete it. It's not supposed to be on my to-do list. It's already on his. Shalom is the peaceful fruit of God's initiative, God's labor, God's faithfulness, and not my own. That wobbly, bumpy, misshapen lump of clay *rests* under the skill of the potter's hands, and as a result it becomes smooth, solid, and centered. And so it is with my soul.

Questions for Reflection and Discussion:

Reflect on your schedule this past week. Was it characterized by joy and peace, ease and strength? Or was it marred by fearful striving? Were you able to find moments of Shalom despite the push and pull of life's circumstances?

Now get specific: What changes do you need to make in your life so that the Great Shalom, the peace of God, is an ever-increasing part of your daily life?

Prayer:

Lord God, I don't want to be tossed to and fro by the screeching demands of my circumstances. I want to rest under your hand, quiet, content, strong, and centered. Rather than trying harder to fix all this, I choose to slow down, breathe deep, open my hands, and let it go. Amen.

6
Opening

The potter presses into the center and opens the clay.

From the potter's point of view, this next step is just about the most beautiful step in the whole process. The clay has been eagerly sought and joyfully found. It has been cleaned and prepared, attached to the wheel. It is perfectly centered. It looks good and it feels good. Smooth. Round. Beautiful.

There is only one problem with this lovely lump of clay. I heard Jon Mourglia say it well in a pottery demonstration he did years ago. He said, "This lump of clay is full of itself!" And he's right. The lump is solid through and through. There is no opening that will turn the lump into a bowl, a cup, a vase. There is no opening into which I may put my Cheerios, pour my coffee, arrange my daffodils. The lump is lovely and it is centered, but at this point in the process, there is too much in the way and it is no use to me at all.

In order to transform that clay into something I can use, I have to open a hole in the middle of it. I rest my left hand lightly on the outside of the clay; I use my right hand to press into the top of the clay. Pressing down and pulling out, I move the clay aside and open up an empty place.

Empty places. How carefully we arrange our lives to make sure we avoid empty places! Unscheduled Friday nights. Long Sunday afternoons. Silent car rides. Quiet living rooms. Still office spaces.

We can hardly stand it. We flip on the television, turn up the radio, crank up our schedules. We overstuff our closets, our desk tops, our calendars. Because, to tell the truth, we hate empty places.

We fill them up as fast as we can with whatever we can get our hands on.

Sometimes we stuff them with sin—we numb the anxious feelings with alcohol, pills, drugs, sensual indulgence.

Or sometimes we just overdo it a little to soothe ourselves—recreational shopping, extra desserts, junky magazines, hour after hour of video games or sports radio.

Or rather than sin or overdo, sometimes we just keep our lives noisy and crowded, filled to overflowing. With good things: service projects, ministry opportunities, wholesome books, visits with friends.

The problem is that we are not very useful when we are full of ourselves. God can fill us and use us only when we clear the way, leave some room, and cultivate an open, empty space.

How do we create empty space? Since emptiness and quiet can be frightening, we might start small, with baby steps. Turn off the radio in the car on the way to work, and use that time to reflect and pray. Resist the temptation to keep the TV on as "background noise" and put on some instrumental music instead. Go for a walk (no phones, no music) and quietly observe the beauty all around us.

Pray, worship, watch, listen. God can speak to us in many ways. In the book of Job, chapters 38 and 40, we read that God answered Job out of the whirlwind. And so he can. But more often, it seems that we must make room in our schedules, our homes, and our hearts so that we may hear his voice (Psalm 116:1), recognize his voice (Judges 18), listen carefully to his voice (Exodus 15:26), pay attention to his voice (Exodus 23:21), and obey his voice (Exodus 19:5).

More often, it seems that we are not so much like Job as like the prophet Elijah, recorded in 1 Kings. God tells Elijah, "Go out and stand on the mountain in the presence of the Lord, for the Lord is about to pass by" (19:11a). Because he knows the Lord and loves the Lord, Elijah quickly responds.

"Then a great and powerful wind tore the mountains apart and shattered the rocks before the Lord, but the Lord was not in the wind. After the wind there was an earthquake, but the Lord was not in the earthquake. After the earthquake came a fire, but the Lord was not in the fire. And after the fire came a gentle whisper. When Elijah heard it, he pulled his cloak over his face and went out and stood at the mouth of the cave" (19:11b-13a). And there he met with God.

Our daily lives are often tossed by wind, touched by fire, shaken from the ground. It is not easy to struggle through it all, pressing in to the quiet place where we can hear the still, small voice of God. There are disciplines that help us to grow in this way; in fact, most of the ancient disciplines of the church are designed to make space in our lives and our souls for God to pour in more of himself. Let me just mention four disciplines that I have found particularly helpful:

Solitude

Solitude is making specific time to be alone, away from other people and from the voices of co-workers, family members, televisions, radios, tapes, CDs, e-mails, books, and articles. It is deliberately taking a retreat all by myself, perhaps a morning in the park, a day trip to the mountains, a weekend at an abbey or cabin or hotel. It may be the very simple discipline of a morning walk three days a week, or an evening habit of sitting in a rocking chair with closed eyes and open heart.

Silence

When I seek solitude, I take a break from other voices. But when I seek silence, I take a break from my own voice. One aspect of it is to just stop talking. I look for occasions when I can go through some part of a day deliberately without talking, not even phone calls or greeting the neighbors. Another aspect of it is to become aware of the chatter in my head—the excuse making, the schedule planning, the hypothetical conversations with other people, the scolding and complaining I do about myself. When I exercise the discipline of silence, I deliberately hush.

Fasting

To fast is to give up food for a time. It reminds me how dependent and needy I really am. I have struggled with fasting as a discipline for a long time because I really don't understand why it is so powerful, why it is so often seen as a necessary dimension of effective prayer. For me, much of the power in fasting is simply this: it forces me pay attention to feelings of emptiness. And when I acknowledge them and fully experience them, I am better able to give them to God rather than stuff them down, ignore them, cover them up, or find some way to medicate myself against them. And when I muster the courage to admit the pain and fear of emptiness, it becomes a means of profound healing.

Releasing

One of the areas of my life that I constantly struggle with is materialism. I like recreational shopping, what some folks call "retail therapy." I like acquiring new things and playing with the things I have. It is easy for my focus to change from heavenly matters to earthly possessions. As an antidote, I regularly go through my belongings and give things away. In the 40 days of Lent, as part of my preparation for Easter, I give away 40 things as a discipline. In preparation for Christmas, I take a day for my heart to "prepare him room," and I go through the house with a big trash bag, gathering up things that I don't really need any more. Then I box them up to donate them to charity.

These four disciplines—solitude, silence, fasting, and releasing—are powerful tools. There are others, and you might take a look at the recommended reading list at the end of this book for suggestions on what to read to learn more about them. Ultimately, each discipline serves the same purpose: creating an empty space into which God can pour those good things he has prepared for us from before the foundation of the world.

Questions for Reflection and Discussion:

To what extent have you filled up your schedule and your heart as a way of avoiding the scary feeling of being empty? Can you identify any specific things that you need to push out of the way in order to make room for the whisper of God?

Search your heart and then your calendar: Can you make specific time for solitude, silence, fasting, and/or releasing sometime in the next month?

Prayer:

God, it is true—I am better at hanging on to things than letting them go. As a result, my life has gotten so crowded that there is little room for the new things that you want to pour into my life. To be honest, there really isn't very much room for you, either. I don't like to admit it, but I am an awful lot like that innkeeper in Bethlehem who crammed his place full to overflowing, and when the King of Glory came to call, there was no room. Forgive my self-indulgence. Heal my fears. And teach me to be available and open to you. Amen.

7
Shaping

The potter uses pressure, inside and out, to shape the clay.

Now it's time for the fancy stuff. This is what we've been waiting for. Every step before this one is preparation; every step after is finishing work. This is the moment of truth.

In shaping a pot, the potter puts one hand on the inside of the pot, one hand on the outside of the pot, and squeezes the clay in-between, moving from the bottom to the top. The clay is stretched, thinned, and directed between the potter's hands.

Usually, the potter starts by pulling the clay into a cylinder and then working on the cylinder section by section to give it shape. The bottom, or *foot* of the pot, may be wide or narrow, straight or slanted. The sides, or *walls*, form the main part of the pot. The potter shapes the *shoulder*, or upper section, and the *neck*, the top section. Finally, he or she will decide upon a finish for the edge, which is called the *lip*.

Each pot is shaped according to the potter's will. One day I might make coffee mugs, cereal bowls, tea pots, or mixing bowls because I need something useful for my kitchen.

Another day I might make a slender vase because I need something beautiful for my living room.

From time to time, the qualities of a particular clay body suggest its own purpose: a delicate *porcelain* becomes a translucent tea cup. Hearty red *earthenware* becomes a chunky, incised flowerpot. A dark chocolate-brown *stoneware* is perfect for a lantern, pierced to let candlelight shine through.

Whether I am creating a pot because there is a need for something to function in my household, or a need for beauty somewhere in my world, a need to express the joy of creativity, or a need to respond sensitively to my materials, I make each pot as I see fit.

And as I work, good clay doesn't argue. In Isaiah 45:9, it says, "Woe to him who quarrels with his Maker.... Does the clay say to the potter, 'What are you making?' "

Do we do that? When God is making choices and issuing directions, do we dig in our heels and say, "Hey! Wait a minute! Exactly what do you think you are doing?"

You want me to do _what_? Gosh, Lord, you don't mean it. Don't you remember what happened last time I tried that? I mean really....

You want me to talk to _who_? Surely, Lord, you don't mean it. Don't you remember what they did to me last week? After all....

You want me to go _where_? No, that can't possibly be right. Are you sure you know what you're talking about? Think about it this way....

You wanted that done _when_? If only you understood, Lord, how inconvenient your timing is. You really have to consider....

I have heard that you can say "no" or you can say "Lord," but you cannot say "No, Lord" and mean it. It's one or the other. Either God is our Lord and we say yes to his will in his time in his way, or he is not Lord, and we say no to what he is calling us to.

Jonah was given a very clear command to go to Nineveh and preach good news (1:2). He heard exactly what God told him and understood it unequivocally. And he ran the other way.

Ananias, on the other hand, responded righteously. In Acts 9:10-11, we are told that God came to him with a very clear command to go to Damascus and speak good news: "There was a disciple named Ananias. The Lord called to him in a vision, 'Ananias!'

'Yes, Lord,' he answered.

The Lord told him, 'Go to the house of Judas on Straight Street and ask for a man from Tarsus named Saul, for he is praying. In a vision he has seen a man named Ananias come and place his hands on him to restore his sight.' "

House of Judas. Okay. Straight Street. Okay. Laying on of hands. Okay. Restore his sight. Sounds good. Um, wait a minute, Lord. Did you say *Saul of Tarsus*?

The next scene is one of my favorites in all of scripture. Ananias is one of my heroes of the faith—I relate to him more than I relate to most other Bible characters. That's because most of the time, I am not like Jonah, seized by fear and quick to flee in the opposite direction. But I am not like Samuel, either, who hears God and quietly says, "Speak, for your servant is listening." Or the prophet Isaiah, who hears God and instantly responds, "Here I am. Send me."

Instead, I am a lot like Ananias, who loves God and hears God and then needs a little time to sort it out and get it right. There is a difference between arguing with God and talking things out. When God tells him to go and pray for Saul of Tarsus, Ananias thinks that maybe God is a little bit confused and needs a few things pointed out to him: "'Lord,' Ananias answered, 'I have heard many reports about this man and all the harm he has done to your saints in Jerusalem. And he has come here with authority from the chief priests to arrest all who call on your name'" (vs.13-14).

Listen, God. Haven't you been following the news? Didn't you read the latest *Jerusalem Post*? This Saul character? He's a bad one. This is a foolish thing you are calling me to do! Are you *sure* you know what you are asking?

I don't think Ananias is being resistant. I don't think he is being disobedient. After all, he prefaces his words with the declaration *LORD*. This command just doesn't make any sense to him, and so he wants to clarify things, wants to be sure. Mary does the same thing when the angel announces that she will be the mother of the messiah: I am available, she says, but I really don't understand. Please, can you explain how this thing is going to work?

God answers honest questions and honors those who seek him by addressing their concerns.

"But the Lord said to Ananias, 'Go! This man is my chosen instrument to carry my name before the Gentiles and their kings and before the people of Israel.'" Then God adds, "I will show him how much he must suffer for my name" (vs.15-16).

So Ananias went.

We don't always know why God shapes one person one way, another person another way. Why a life takes a turn in an unexpected direction, why a plan goes awry, why a dream is marred, why a goal is thwarted. I believe that God loves to take the time to talk with us about those things that are troubling our hearts. But here's the catch: he is still Lord. He may graciously take the time to reason with us. He may explain things with great clarity and purpose. Or he may be stubbornly silent on the matter. In either case, at some point or another he will say, "Go!" And that's exactly what we must do.

Questions for Reflection and Discussion:

Think about the shape of your past. Is there an unexpected turn of events that didn't make sense at the time, but now is a clear indication of God's good and perfect will? Share that story with someone this week. It will be an encouragement to them and to you.

Think about the shape of your future. In your heart, are you clear about saying an unconditional "Yes!" to Jesus, the Lord? If you sense a place of resistance, ask for God's help to identify it and understand it and work through it.

Prayer:

Lord, forgive me for all of the times that I have argued, explained, excused, and fought the shaping process in my life. I really do want the shape of my life to reflect your good and perfect will. I really want the shape of my soul to reflect the character and nature of Jesus.

Sometimes I'm not very good at saying yes, Lord. But I want to get better at it. So let me make this declaration now. If you want to make my life into something that is useful to your kingdom, take me. I've said no, maybe, later, we'll see. Today I say, "Yes, Lord."

And tomorrow when I wake, pour out a fresh batch of grace so that I have all that I need to say yes, Lord, again.

Thank you for loving me enough to keep forming and shaping and molding and working in my life, day by day by day. Amen.

8
Restoring

If the clay pot weakens, wobbles, and collapses, God is not daunted.

The Old Testament prophets really had it rough.

What about poor Ezekiel? Has to draw a picture of Jerusalem and then lie down on his left side for 390 days. And then bake bread out of wheat, barley, beans, lentils, millet and spelt, and cook it over cow dung (Ezekiel 4).

What about poor Ahijah? Buys a brand new cloak and then God tells him to tear it into twelve pieces and start handing them out (1 Kings 11:29-39).

What about poor Jeremiah? Buries his new linen belt in the dirt (Jeremiah 13). Gets tossed in a cistern (Jeremiah 38). Has a vision of rotten figs (Jeremiah 24).

God constantly uses vivid pictures to teach his people spiritual lessons. So God talks to the prophet Jeremiah about potters and clay. God tells him to go down to the potter's house, "and there I will give you my message" (Jeremiah 18:2). Jeremiah obeys. He watches the potter working on the wheel, and as we have seen, there are many things about this experience that are vivid, powerful, relevant, impacting.

But this time, as Jeremiah watches the potter and the clay, something goes terribly wrong: "The pot he was shaping from the clay was marred in his hands" (Jeremiah 18:4a). What went wrong? What would cause a pot to "become marred" in the hands of the potter?

It could be that one of those impurities, one of those bumps or bubbles, came to the surface and knocked things off center.

It could be that one of those wobbles, so tiny at the centering stage, became bigger and bigger until the whole thing started to lean and then toppled right over.

Let's assume that the clay was clean, the centering was done correctly, and the potter was both skillful and careful. Even with all of that going for it, the pot may still be marred.

There are lots of things that can cause it, but one of the most common causes of damage at this point is called *clay fatigue*. That's right, fatigue. If the clay is pulled and stretched too much, water seeps in between the flat plates that make up the clay, and the water weakens its structure. Too many pulls, too much time, too much moisture, and the water will weaken the clay so much that the pot will simply flop over. Clay fatigue.

Ever felt like you've been pulled one time too many, and simply flopped right over?

Ever had one of those days?

Here is the good news. If the pot becomes marred at this point in the process, it is fairly easy for the potter to make things right.

The clay is still moist, soft, resilient. The potter scoops it up, pats it into a ball, and walks over to the wedging table. Working with it in much the same way a baker works with dough, the potter wedges the clay, pressing and turning, eliminating pockets of air, softening dry places, bringing strength and integrity to the entire lump of clay. Once the clay has been thoroughly wedged, the potter returns to the wheel, firmly attaches it to the wheel head, sets the wheel to spinning, and simply starts all over again.

When the pot comes tumbling down, it may seem like a disaster. But the potter is never daunted. There is always something he can do.

Questions for Reflection and Discussion:

Fatigue is a fact of life for most of us. Consider if there is a need in your life right now to make changes that will bring refreshment and prevent the destruction to mind and body that comes from accumulated fatigue. Then consider: Is someone you know facing serious challenges in the push and pull of life? Is there something you (or your small group) can do this week to reduce the stress and help carry the load?

Think of a time when you have faced a major setback—when things did not go smoothly, when the process was interrupted with an unexpected collapse. Do you have a testimony of the way that God can move into a situation, and start all over again?

Prayer:

Identify one particular situation that seems beyond repair.

Then pray:

Lord, I just can't see how this situation could possibly be made right. Give me the strength to scoop up this soft and soggy mess, put it in your loving hands, and trust you to make it right again. Amen.

9 Persisting

The pot is taken off the wheel and left to dry.

As the potter finishes shaping the pot, several tools are used. A sponge might be used to smooth the surface and finish the upper edge or the lip. A needle tool might be used to trim the top or shape the very bottom, where extra clay might have accumulated between the pot and the wheel head. A small, flat piece of wood or plastic or metal, called a *rib*, might be used to give final shape to the neck or shoulder or body of the pot.

Once the shaping process is complete, the potter removes the pot from the wheel. A thin piece of wire is held taut between the potter's fingers, and slid in-between the bottom of the pot and the surface of the wheel head. The pot is lifted from the wheel, put on a flat board, and set on a shelf to dry.

I don't know what pots are thinking, but sometimes I imagine that this is a pretty scary stage in the life of that pot. After enduring so much pressure and experiencing such close, careful attention from the potter, now all of a sudden the pot is cut loose, pulled away from the wheel, set aside, and left alone. Pressure and pulling are uncomfortable, but what is this sudden isolation, sudden stillness, sudden loneliness? Have I been abandoned? Have I been rejected? Did I do something wrong? Is this the end of my story?

It is like the forty days that Jesus spent in the wilderness early in his ministry. When we remember this story, we don't actually think much about the forty days at all. In our minds, we tend to go immediately to day forty-one. Satan appears and presents the Lord with three temptations. Jesus overcomes each one by quoting scripture. Man does not live by bread alone! Worship the Lord God and serve him only! Do not put the Lord God to the test! (Luke 4:1-13). It is dramatic. Christ is triumphant. And it is the climactic event that launches him into public ministry.

But what about that period of forty long days? Forty days. That's more than a month without food, without friends. What was happening in that desert time? Didn't the hours seem awfully long? Wasn't the pace awfully slow? Weren't his patience and his perseverance tested day after day, long before the devil arrived on the scene? And in some ways, weren't those days of testing just as difficult because they were not nearly so dramatic?

What is both hard to remember and important to understand is that times of waiting are not accidental. God's watch is not broken, his timing is not tardy, his purpose is not lost, his work is not abandoned, his promise is not forgotten. The great saints have always faced times when they wondered and waited. Abraham and Sarah sitting childless in their tent. Joseph languishing in Pharaoh's prison. Moses tending sheep in the desert for more than forty years. Ruth gleaning in the fields day after day after day. Nehemiah worrying about the condition of Jerusalem's walls. Waiting. Not much going on. Hope once burned big and bright, but now? Now it's all ashes and wondering.

But God has not forgotten, and he is "not slow in keeping his promise, as some understand slowness" (2 Peter 3:9a). The example of the clay makes this clear. The potter has not forgotten the pot. The pot has been set aside *on purpose*, that a particular work be accomplished in it. Through sitting and waiting.

This time of waiting is absolutely necessary. The pot must dry completely, top to bottom, through and through. If there is any moisture hidden in the wall of the pot, there will be trouble when the pot is fired. That is because water heats up much faster than clay. As the kiln gets hotter, the water will turn to steam and explode out of the side of the pot. The pot will be split apart and all this careful work will be for nothing.

So the pot is left to sit and wait until it is absolutely dry, through and through. It is brought to a state known as *bone dry*.

Waiting. Sitting. Silent. Untouched. Unnoticed. Until the work is thoroughly finished. This, too, is a necessary part of the process.

Questions for Reflection and Discussion:

Is there a time in your life when a project has been ruined or compromised because you were impatient and skipped some steps along the way? Ask God to forgive you, and then ask him to show you what you might learn from the experience.

Is there a particular project or event or issue in your life right now that seems to be on hold? Find someone to pray with this week and seek God's direction concerning it. With the help of a trusted friend, seek to discern if now is the time for things to change, or if this is a time to wait. Patiently. For the fullness of time. Until this stage of the process is truly completed.

Prayer:

God, I have the fidgets. I don't like to sit and wait. I don't really trust the dry times when nothing seems to be happening. Help me to grow in trust and patience so that I can understand what John Milton meant when he wrote, "They also serve who only stand and wait." Amen.

10 Renewing

If the bone dry pot is chipped, cracked, or dropped, God is not daunted.

During this dry time, the pot is extremely vulnerable: even gentle handling can cause chips, splits, and cracks. This lesson really came alive to me as we were preparing the photographs for this book. My photographer worked with me through all the stages of pottery making. He toured the ceramics studio. He watched me select and prepare the clay. He took pictures as I attached, centered, opened, and pulled several pots. And he handled and took pictures of pots in many shapes and sizes, pots I had made, and pots made by others.

In particular, he took several pictures of a large, beautiful vase, made by Susan Ney. The pot was bone dry.

There was only one problem: he didn't know that it was bone dry. He thought it had already been fired. As we finished the photo shoot and started cleaning up, he grabbed this beautiful vase by the inside of the lip and swung around to take it back to its shelf inside the studio.

That vase crumbled to pieces in his hand. I walked by just seconds after it happened—his eyes were as wide as saucers and the broken bits covered the ground around his feet.

"I—I don't understand. I was so careful..." he started. And that's true. He had been.

But that pot was bone dry. Even the most careful handling at this point can cause everything to fall to pieces.

Here is the good news. If the pot becomes marred at this point in the process, it is a fairly easy matter for the potter to make things right.

If the break is small, the pot can be repaired. A chipped lip can be smoothed. A bumped handle can be reattached.

If the damage is more extensive, the process takes a little longer. The dry pieces are soaked in water (remember that water is a picture of the Holy Spirit). The clay dissolves and returns to its soft, resilient state. The potter scoops it up, wedges it, reattaches it to the wheel head, and starts the shaping process all over again.

A good potter can take that very same clay and make that very same pot all over again.

A very good potter can take that very same clay and make something even better.

Better? Better. God can pick up the broken pieces of our lives, our ministries, our hearts, our hopes, our dreams. He can saturate them in the power of the Holy Spirit so that they are no longer tense, tight, fragile, and brittle. Those pieces become soft, resilient, and pliable, just like they used to be. And God, the Master Potter, can make that very same pot all over again. Or maybe, just maybe, he will make something even better.

When we understand this principle, we see that dry pots become dry bones, just waiting for new life. It is like another powerful picture, one that God gave to the prophet Ezekiel:

> The hand of the Lord was upon me, and he brought me out by the Spirit of the Lord and set me in the middle of a valley; it was full of bones. He led me back and forth among them, and I saw a great many bones on the floor of the valley, bones that were very dry.
>
> He asked me, "Son of man, can these bones live?"
>
> I said, "O Sovereign Lord, you alone know."
>
> Then he said to me, "Prophesy to these bones and say to them, 'Dry bones, hear the word of the Lord! This is what the Sovereign Lord says to these bones: I will make breath enter you, and you will come to life. I will attach tendons to you and make flesh come upon you and cover you with skin; I will put breath in you, and you will come to life. Then you will know that I am the Lord.'"
>
> So I prophesied as I was commanded. And as I was prophesying, there was a noise, a rattling sound, and the bones came together, bone to bone. I looked, and tendons and

flesh appeared on them and skin covered them, but there was no breath in them.

Then he said to me, "Prophesy to the breath; prophesy, son of man, and say to it, 'This is what the Sovereign Lord says: Come from the four winds, O breath, and breathe into these slain, that they may live.'"

So I prophesied as he commanded me, and breath entered them; they came to life. (Ezekiel 37:1-10a)

New life for old, dry bones. It is one of the most powerful pictures in the Bible. It is one of the most beautiful promises of God. It is available for you.

Questions for Reflection and Discussion:

Do you have broken pieces of some situation, some life dream, some relationship, some gift or ability that seems broken beyond repair? Give the pieces to God in prayer—and see what he will do.

After my photographer broke that pot, he went to the potter and quickly apologized and offered to make restitution. She responded graciously, with strong words of forgiveness and encouragement. Is there something that you have broken but have not yet made right—a promise, a commitment, perhaps a possession? Even when we are careful, our words and actions can be destructive, and we need to do everything in our power to make things right. Are there things that you need to do this week to make amends?

Prayer:

For this prayer time, let me pray this prayer over you:

Sovereign Lord, in the life and heart of this precious one, there are many bones and they are very dry. There are disappointments and injuries of every kind. There are dreams that have died. There are people who have been lost. There are relationships broken. There are hopes dashed. There are longings that have remained unfulfilled.

O God, let these bones live. Restore, revive, refresh. Breathe on them, Breath of Life. Make them new. Amen.

11 Transforming

The pot is gathered up, put into the kiln, and fired.

As the pot waits and dries, it must be tedious and tiresome, at least at first. But after a while, I wonder if that pot doesn't settle in and get pretty comfortable. It is nice and quiet, after all. The potter seems to have gone off somewhere and left the pot to its own devices. So maybe the pot figures that since it's been left to fend for itself, it'll just make the best of it.

The owner of the vineyard leaves, and the tenants are left to steward the property (Mark 12).

The master goes on a journey, and the workers are entrusted with the careful use of their talents (Matthew 25).

The bridegroom is delayed and the waiting virgins are expected to keep their lamps trim and bright (Matthew 25).

But after a while, the tenants start to get selfish, the workers start to get lazy, the young girls get a little sleepy. Luke warns us that we are wise to keep watch, stay ready. "It will be good for those servants whose master finds them watching when he comes" (12:37a). Waiting patiently is one thing. Waiting expectantly, alert and prepared, is even better.

Because suddenly, without warning, time's up.

The potter picks the pot off the shelf and stacks it in a kiln. The kiln may be large or small. It may be powered by gas, electricity, or wood. No matter its size or kind, the purpose of the kiln is to heat the pot to about a thousand degrees Fahrenheit. The firing process heats the clay so hot that a permanent change takes place. The clay becomes very hard through a process called *quartz inversion*: the silica in the clay changes in volume due to the extreme heat. After it is fired, the pot is smaller, lighter, and much, much stronger. Fired clay is permanent: it will no longer dissolve in water.

It is interesting to me that pots are shaped alone but they go through the fire together. After drying, the pots are crowded together, stacked on top of one another, nestled inside each other. In a similar way, God often gives us companions in the fiery trials of life, companions who can pray with us, talk with us, stand with us.

That was the case with Shadrach, Meshach and Abednego. We read in the third chapter of Daniel that Nebuchadnezzar became furious with Shadrach, Meshach and Abednego because they refused to bow down to the idol he had made. So the king took action: "He ordered the furnace heated seven times hotter than usual and commanded some of the strongest soldiers in his army to tie up Shadrach, Meshach and Abednego and throw them into the blazing furnace" (Daniel 3:19b-20).

We have looked at difficult times in the process of making a pot. The pot is cleaned, wedged, stretched, and dried. Now comes the very worst of it: the pot is flung into the blazing furnace. Hot. Very hot. Impossibly hot. "The king's command was so urgent and the furnace so hot that the flames of the fire killed the men who took up Shadrach, Meshach and Abednego, and these three men, firmly tied, fell into the blazing furnace" (3:22-23).

The fire is hot and the fire is dangerous. It can bring about great harm. But although our enemies, and the Enemy of our Souls, may intend the fire for great harm, our God is able to use it to bring about great good.

The one who is tested comes forth as fine gold (Job 23:10).

The one who is pruned bears much fruit (John 15:2).

The pot that is fired is made strong and useful.

Think about it. If I put hot coffee or cold milk or ice water into an unfired clay vessel, the whole thing will dissolve into a big old pile of mush. It hasn't been tested, hasn't been tried. It hasn't been made strong in the fire. So while it may *look* very attractive, it really can't be used. It's not good for anything. Not until it is transformed by fire.

The process isn't easy and it isn't comfortable. But one thing we can count on is that Christ will meet us in the midst of it all. Think again of Shadrach, Meshach and Abednego:

> Then King Nebuchadnezzar leaped to his feet in amazement and asked his advisors, "Wasn't it three men that we tied up and threw into the fire?"
>
> They replied, "Certainly, O king."
>
> He said, "Look! I see four men walking around in the fire, unbound and unharmed, and the fourth looks like a son of the gods."
>
> Nebuchadnezzar then approached the opening of the blazing furnace and shouted, "Shadrach, Meshach and Abednego, servants of the Most High God, come out! Come here!"
>
> So Shadrach, Meshach and Abednego came out of the fire, and the satraps, prefects, governors and royal advisers crowded around them. They saw that the fire had not harmed their bodies, nor was a hair of their heads singed; their robes were not scorched, and there was no smell of fire on them.
>
> Then Nebuchadnezzar said, "Praise be to the God of Shadrach, Meshach and Abednego, who has sent his angel and rescued his servants! They trusted in him and defied the king's command and were willing to give up their lives rather than serve or worship any god except their own God." (Daniel 3:24-28)

Praise be to the God of Shadrach, Meshach and Abednego! Nebuchadnezzar saw it clearly: "no other God can save in this way" (3:29b). The fire is hot and the trial is hard. But in the end, God is glorified and God's people are made strong.

How should we respond when fiery trials come? I don't much like the answer. But here it is, straight from the book of James: "Consider it pure joy, my brothers, whenever you face trials of many kinds, because you know that the testing of your faith develops perseverance. Perseverance must finish its work so that you may be mature and complete, not lacking anything" (1:2-4).

Questions for Reflection and Discussion:

What does it mean to you to be prepared, alert, ready for the return of the master and prepared for whatever trials may come? In what ways does your life reflect this readiness? In what ways might you adjust your day to better reflect this awareness?

Thank God for those who have stood by you during fiery trials. Then thank them: take time this week to write a note or make a call saying thank you to someone who has stood by you in tough times.

Prayer:

Dear God. Consider my trials *pure joy*? Hmmm. I'm not there quite yet. But I'm learning, Lord, to accept good times and bad times as gifts from your hand. I'm learning to ask, "What is God saying to me in the midst of this circumstance?" And I'm starting to see that these things happen for a reason, that they can help to accomplish important things in my life, and that no matter how hot the fire gets, you mean it when you say that you will NEVER leave me, you will NEVER forsake me. I'm learning, Lord. Help me to learn it better. Help me to live it more. Amen.

12 Repairing

If the fired pot is knocked over, cracked, dropped, or broken, God is not daunted.

A pot that has been fired once is very, very strong. When I do pottery workshops, there is one part of my demonstration that I particularly enjoy. I bring two pots with me, one of them made of dry, unfired clay, called *greenware*, and one of them made of clay that has been fired once, called *bisqueware*. They look almost identical.

I take the greenware pot. I give it to the most delicate and precious woman I can find: an elderly saint, a very young child. "Crush it," I say. And she looks at me, bewildered.

"Crush it."

One little squeeze, and that pot crumbles.

I take the bisqueware pot. I give it to the biggest, strongest, heartiest man I can find: a football player, a construction worker. "Crush it," I say. And he looks at me, grinning.

But the job is not so easy. He squeezes, stammers, grits his teeth, squeezes some more. Finally he resorts to one of two approaches: he either pulls it apart with both hands, or he slaps it against something hard and it shatters.

Yes, he manages to break it. But it really takes some doing. As a result of so much attention from the potter and so much heat from the flame, the pot is far stronger and more durable than ever before. It is well on its way to becoming something beautiful and useful.

But can anything be done if a fired pot gets broken? As we saw earlier, if the pot has never been fired, the potter simply gathers up the broken pieces and adds water. The hard, dry clay dissolves, and the potter simply starts the process all over again.

Fired clay is different. It has been permanently, unalterably, forever changed. Time has passed. And trials. It is rigid now. Strong. Hard. Water can't touch it. It won't dissolve.

What if something really bad happens at this stage of the pot's life, and the pot is somehow chipped, or split, or crushed?

A small chip, crack, or break can still be mended. It requires careful work, but the broken bits can be gathered up, dusted off, reattached, and smoothed over. A very strong bonding material can be used—so strong, in fact, that the bonded place becomes stronger than the pot itself. If the pot is subjected to stress again, it will not break in the place that has been repaired. It becomes strongest in the broken places.

What if the pot is completely split apart, or if the shattered pieces can no longer be gathered together? It, too, can be mended or reused. But before we consider that process, it is worth remembering that it may be in brokenness that a pot achieves its highest purpose.

A great battle is won.

In Judges 7, we read about Gideon and his small army, ready to defend Israel by overcoming the Midianites. It seems impossible, and the Lord's battle strategy is very unusual. Gideon divides his three hundred men into three companies. Then, "he placed trumpets and empty jars in the hands of all of them, with torches inside" (7:16b). No swords or muskets, no rifles or bayonets. Trumpets. Torches. And clay jars. And just watch what happens next:

> Gideon and the hundred men with him reached the edge of the camp at the beginning of the middle watch, just after they had changed the guard. They blew their trumpets and broke the jars that were in their hands. The three companies blew the trumpets and smashed the jars. Grasping the torches in their left hands and holding in their right hands the trumpets they were to blow, they shouted, "A sword for the Lord and for Gideon!" While each man held his position around the camp, all the Midianites ran, crying out as they fled. (7:19-21)

God won a great victory that day. And clay vessels, broken to reveal the light, were the means used by God to accomplish it.

A great honor is bestowed.

In Mark 14:3, we read about an extravagant act of worship and sacrifice: "While [Jesus] was in Bethany, reclining at the table in the home of a man known as Simon the leper, a woman came with an alabaster jar of very expensive perfume, made of pure nard. She broke the jar and poured the perfume on his head." Jesus is honored by this act and says, "She has done a beautiful thing to me." She breaks the costly container and pours out the entire contents. C. S. Lewis understood the significance of this passage. In his book *Letters to an American Lady,* Lewis writes, "The allegorical sense of her great action dawned on me the other day. The precious alabaster box which one must *break* over the Holy Feet is one's *heart.* Easier said than done. And the contents become perfume only when it is broken."

The psalmist adds, "The sacrifices of God are a broken spirit; a broken and contrite heart, O God, you will not despise" (51:17).

Jesus is anointed in preparation for what is to come. And the alabaster jar, broken to pour out its contents, was the means used by God to accomplish it.

A great deliverance is accomplished.

The greatest moment in all of human history is a moment of brokenness. Christ willingly offered himself on the cross, a perfect sacrifice for the whole world. He knew in advance that this was the significance of his death: "The Lord Jesus, on the night he was betrayed, took bread, and when he had given thanks, he broke it and said, 'This is my body, which is for you'" (1 Corinthians 11:23b-24). It is brokenness that we honor every time we take communion together (1 Corinthians 10:16).

God accomplished redemption that day. And the body of Christ, broken for you, was the means used by God to accomplish it.

There is one other image in pottery that helps to emphasize the beauty of brokenness. Even if the fired pot is completely crushed, it is not too late to redeem it. Even in the face of complete destruction, God is not daunted.

When potters want to create a work that is particularly challenging—especially thin, unusually tall, creative in shape, risky in form—they add a powdery material called *grog* to the wet clay. Grog gives the soft clay added strength and body, allowing it to be pushed farther and pulled harder than it would otherwise. Clay *without* grog is more likely to fatigue and flop. Clay *with* grog is better able to withstand challenges, repeated stresses, and unusually difficult work.

Grog is made up of fired clay that has been broken up and then ground into a gritty powder.

In terms of structure, grog supports the clay body by adding extra strength and solidity that new clay simply doesn't have.

But in terms of imagery, grog is a picture of how experience through the tough times of life gives strength in the midst of brand new challenges. When you add old grog to new clay, it's almost as if the gift of strength gained through brokenness and suffering is communicated to the newer, younger vessels.

It's like the dear saints in your church who have been through tough times, and because of it have so much to offer to the health and effectiveness of your congregation. It's like the single mother who has raised a fine family and now is able to come alongside the teenager who is pregnant and afraid. It's like the man who once knew the bondage of alcoholism and ended up on the streets, now sober and able to relate powerfully to others who face the same temptations.

In our families, our neighborhoods, our fellowships, our small groups, there are individuals all around us who bring the grit of real experience that gives lasting strength to us all.

Questions for Reflection and Discussion:

Is there a ministry you have now that is a result of hardship in your past? Is there a ministry you might enter into now that builds upon the strength of your experiences for the benefit of others?

Are there worries, fears, needs, longings, injuries, or other treasures locked tight inside your heart, things that need to be broken open and poured out at the feet of Jesus? Do it in a way that you find meaningful: pray, worship, journal, talk, sing, create, walk, cry, dance, sew, paint, plant. Is this best addressed through time alone, through some activity, through words, or through personal time with a trusted friend or counselor or minister?

Prayer:

Lord Jesus, everything in me wants to avoid the sacrifice of brokenness. But I'm beginning to see that much can be accomplished *because* of brokenness, not just in spite of it. Gideon's torches couldn't shine bright until the jars were shattered. Sweet anointing oil couldn't be spread on your feet until the box was crushed. And I know that the ultimate example is your own sacrifice, your body broken for me. Help me, Lord, to see how the pain and difficulty of my life can be a source of strength and healing for myself, and for others. Help me to understand the great mystery of Philippians 3:10, the fellowship of your suffering that leads to the power of your resurrection. Amen.

13 Returning

The pot is glazed and goes back into the fire.

Several years ago, my husband and I bought a small house, the kind that is called a "fixer-upper." It was tiny and shabby and adorable. I couldn't wait to begin the transformation process, to roll up my sleeves and see how God might make a mountain of glory out of this little molehill. Two days after we moved in, I headed for the back yard with toolbox in hand. The first job was to scrape off the years of grime and old paint from the windows and let the sun shine through. So I grabbed a razor tool in my right hand.

But I grabbed it too quickly, too carelessly. It slipped, and the corner of the blade slid into the knuckle of my little finger. The wound was quick and very deep.

The orthopedic surgeon told me that I had severed the tendon of that finger, and that he would have to open up my hand and reattach the tendon. He rushed me to the hospital, and as I waited in the prep room for surgery, the anesthesiologist and nurse sat with me and talked to me about the procedure. I was relaxed, even cheerful. They seemed puzzled by that, but the explanation was simple: I had never had any kind of surgery before. I had never even been hospitalized before. I had no idea what I was in for.

If I had to go through surgery again, knowing what I know now about how difficult and painful it is—about the months of recovery, the difficulty of physical therapy, the disfiguring effect of that long, pink scar—I might not be so cavalier about it all. I was brave only because I had no idea how hard it would be.

Clay that has never been fired is a little bit like that. The potter lifts the pot and loads it into the kiln. The clay has absolutely no idea what it is in for. To say yes to the first firing is not such a big deal.

But to go through the fire a second time is another matter altogether. Been there. Done that. Hated every minute of it. But sometimes that is exactly what we are called to do. Go back. And do it again.

Going to an estranged brother again and again and again, risking the pain of rejection because there is some faint hope that reconciliation might be possible. And still persisting.

Going to the nursing home week after week after week to visit an ailing parent who never seems to get better but is losing both awareness and ability as time goes by. And still persisting.

Going to a tiresome job day after day after day, even though it is not rewarding or fulfilling in any way. And still persisting.

Returning to a place of pain and challenge is never easy.

Joseph's brothers knew it. When the famine was great in Israel, ten of Joseph's brothers went to Egypt to buy grain (Genesis 42). It was a long, dusty journey, and when they arrived, they had a strange and stressful interaction with Joseph who "pretended to be a stranger and spoke harshly to them" (vs. 7). Putting Egypt behind them, they returned to Israel and to their father Jacob. But it wasn't long before their need became severe once more. Do they dare another trip to Egypt? Yes, they do. And ultimately they are reunited with their brother.

Nehemiah knew it. When the walls of Jerusalem had fallen into disrepair, Nehemiah led a great initiative and rebuilt the walls and the gates of the great city (Nehemiah 1-6). More than forty-two thousand Hebrew exiles returned, and Jerusalem experienced a glorious rebirth (Nehemiah 7-12). His work complete, Nehemiah returned to Babylon, and while he was gone, things completely fell apart. Does he dare another attempt to restore that city? Yes, he does. And ultimately he sees God's word triumph.

Moses knew it. When the Hebrews crossed the Red Sea into freedom, they needed God's guidance to give order to their lives. So God met with Moses on Mount Sinai: "The smoke billowed up from it like smoke from a furnace, the whole mountain trembled violently, and the sound of the trumpet grew louder and louder" (Exodus 19:18b). God wrote his law on stone tablets. Putting Sinai behind him, Moses walked back into camp. Seeing the golden calf, he was enraged and broke the tablets to pieces. Then God came to him a second time: "Chisel out two stone tablets like the first ones, and I will write on them the words that were on the first tablets" (Exodus 34:1). Does he dare another meeting with the God of smoke and trembling? Yes, he does. And ultimately the full law of God is faithfully given.

For the clay pot, the second time through the kiln is the step that brings out its full beauty. Before the pot is fired the second time, it is glazed. A thick suspension of chemicals, basically tiny, tiny, tiny bits of glass, is brushed on the surface. As the temperature rises, these melt and fuse together, covering the pot in bright color.

The first time brings out the strength of the pot.

The second time brings out its color and its true beauty.

But it takes courage, lots of courage, to go back and go through it again. Back to Egypt. Back to Jerusalem. Back to Mount Sinai. Back into the fire and flame. The second trip is infinitely harder than the first. But in the background is a whisper, a promise: "The Lord is the everlasting God, the Creator of the ends of the earth. He will not grow tired or weary, and his understanding no one can fathom. He gives strength to the weary and increases the power of the weak. Even youths grow tired and weary, and young men stumble and fall; but those who hope in the Lord will renew their strength. They will soar on wings like eagles; they will run and not grow weary, they will walk and not be faint" (Isaiah 40:28b-31).

Questions for Reflection and Discussion:

Is there some task that you have been afraid to face because you have been there before and it is too painful to imagine trying it again? Talk to God about it, and ask for the courage to persist in doing what is right.

Is there some ongoing task that has become very nearly unbearable, but still you sense the need to stay and faithfully complete it? Ask God to transform the mundane into the miraculous so that you can see his hand even in the midst of this circumstance.

Prayer:

God, there are things in my life that are difficult because I really have counted the cost and experienced the pain and that makes it harder for me to persevere. I pray that you would either change my heart or change my circumstances. And whichever it is that you choose to do, I am determined to look for the ways that love, joy, peace, patience, kindness, goodness, faithfulness, gentleness, and self-control will abound in my life. Amen.

CLAY IN THE POTTER'S HANDS

14

Redeeming

If the finished pot is dropped and shattered, God is not daunted.

There it sits, bright and beautiful, on the dining room table holding fresh flowers, in the china cabinet waiting for a company meal, on your desk at work offering a spot of beauty in the midst of the daily routine of life. Our pot is finished.

So let's imagine the unimaginable.

What happens if this strong, colorful, beautiful, finished pot is dropped?

Even now, even at this point in the process, it is still possible for the potter to make things right.

Several years ago, I began experimenting with a new art form: mosaic. I had seen examples of mosaic, small and large, and was attracted to the beauty of it all.

There is a restaurant not far from my house with an exquisite entryway made entirely out of large, richly colored pieces of broken pottery, arranged in a bright, bold abstract design.

There is a fountain in a neighborhood courtyard, and the fountain is covered with very small pieces of colorful ceramic tiles.

I have seen ancient mosaics in museums, some of them more than twelve feet high, and they contain complex images of people, horses, battles, columns, and other stirring scenes. After thousands of years, the colors are still astonishingly bright, clear, strong, and beautiful.

Even the ceramic tiles that you might find in your bathroom wall or your kitchen counter or the floor of your front hall are a kind of mosaic, beautiful, durable surfaces made up of smaller pieces of glazed and fired clay.

Those large, ancient mosaics in the museum and the bright, modern trim in the restaurant are made through very similar processes. A clean, smooth surface is prepared, and the small ceramic pieces are arranged in a pattern. Once the pattern is determined, each individual piece is glued into place. Then grout is applied over the entire thing. Grout looks and feels a lot like cake frosting. It is worked into all of the cracks in between the pieces and then smoothed out. Then the surface of each clay piece is carefully wiped clean with a damp sponge. After the grout hardens, in a few hours or a day or two, the clay tiles are buffed with a soft cloth to remove every trace of grout from their surface, and to let the color shine.

Since I am a potter, I like to use broken dishes when I make mosaics. I take broken tea cups and dinner plates and soup bowls and combine the parts in new ways to decorate a bird house or flower pot or table top. As I work, I am reminded of the miracle of redemption. I have a friend who is a quilter. She uses bits of fabric in much the same way as I use bits of clay, joining old scraps together in new ways, making something of beauty and great worth.

The original ceramic piece served one purpose, and it was good in its season. The brand new ceramic piece will serve its purpose, too. And it is good in its season.

It is interesting to me that when my students and my friends found out that I was making mosaics, they started to bring me chipped bowls, split plates, cracked statuary, broken coffee mugs. Every now and then I would arrive at work in the morning to find a grocery bag filled with old pottery sitting in front of my office door! There have been serving platters in my mailbox, porcelain lovebirds on my desk, sacks of old, unmatched saucers on my rocking chair. One dear friend has taken to prowling estate sales and flea markets searching for chipped china. Another friend used the opportunity to buy herself a whole new set of dishes and give me her old place settings for eight! Each piece, broken into chunks and combined with other shards and cast-offs, has become the raw material for something brand new.

It is especially interesting to me to hear my friends say that knowing about this art form has really changed their perspective. Before, when a dish was dropped or a cup got chipped, they would spit and fume. What a disaster! Now when pottery pieces get broken, they smile: "Wow, look at that. I wonder what Diana can make out of this one?" They see the accident as an opportunity to make a contribution to an artistic cause. It's interesting, isn't it, that the situation didn't change. Just their attitude and point of view.

Rightly understood, there is no raw material, no accident, no broken pieces, that our Creator God can't redeem. Because no matter what, God is never, ever, ever daunted.

Questions for Reflection and Discussion:

List several situations where you have told yourself, "It's too late." Then offer the list to God in prayer.

Take time this week to appreciate the beauty of a mosaic, a quilt, a collage, a scrapbook page, or another art form that is made when an artist redeems bits and pieces by making something brand new. Or set aside time to use your own creative gifts in a new way.

Prayer:

Change my heart, O God, so that I may learn to be always alert to the redemptive opportunities that can be found in even the sorriest mess. Amen.

15
Abiding

The pot is now strong, beautiful, and useful, ready for the Master's use.

It has been a long journey from the stillness of the mountainside, where thick deposits of clay were hidden, to the joy of the potter as he found the clay and carried it home, to the patient process of cleaning, wedging, attaching and shaping the clay, to the flash of fire and the final transformation brought about by intensity and perseverance. We have seen how things look when all goes well. We have also seen that our sovereign God is not daunted by those events we think of as mistakes, missteps, sidetracks, and accidents. All these things work together for good!

We are so much like that clay, loved and sought by the Great Artist, brought into his house, shaped as he sees fit. We are, as Paul says, "joyful in hope, patient in affliction, faithful in prayer" (Romans 12:12). It is true that times get hard: "We are hard pressed on every side, but not crushed; perplexed, but not in despair; persecuted, but not abandoned; struck down, but not destroyed" (2 Corinthians 4:8). How is it possible that we live in such hope? Because we know that we are earthen vessels, jars of clay, carrying around the life of Jesus in us as a testimony that the all-surpassing power is from God and definitely not from us (2 Corinthians 4:7).

There are so many ways in which we resemble that clay pot and reflect the process that it has been through under the potter's loving hand. But there are important differences, too. The pot goes through the process once. Then it is finished. As we move through our lives, as living vessels, we find ourselves repeating various stages of the process. Oh, we may be repeating it at a higher level or experiencing it in a different dimension, but throughout our lives we find that God has just a bit more work to do. He needs to reshape and refine us afresh, until that great day when we are like Christ, when we see him face-to-face (1 John 3:2).

In the meantime, where are you today in this ongoing process?

Feeling a little lost, off the beaten path, lying still, feeling alone, wondering, watching, waiting, but not yet alert to the potter's care?

Being cleaned and jostled, separated from worldliness, feeling the debris being pulled from your life, hating the sense of pain, death, and loss on the one hand, welcoming the cleansing touch that brings freedom on the other?

Getting wedged, pushed and pushed and pushed again, having those bumpy spots addressed so that any unevenness is brought to the surface and each part of your life is straightened, aligned, marked by the strength of complete integrity?

Pushed to commitment, no longer allowed to wiggle and waffle, escape doors shutting to the right and left, being challenged to say a decisive *yes* to God's process?

Centering down, letting go of the extraneous things that knock you off course, refining your focus, bringing your will into complete agreement with his will, even in the littlest things?

Opening up, letting go, creating space, allowing times of stillness and solitude for God to speak the truth to the center of your soul?

Shaping, adapting, adjusting, moving, heading in directions you didn't expect, facing decisions you didn't anticipate, watching your life redirected in scary, surprising, fulfilling, even miraculous ways?

Waiting, still, feeling dry, tempted to be impatient, wondering when it will be time for your breakthrough?

Surprised by the fire, the intensity, the heat, the challenge, the pain, the disappointment?

Frightened by the prospect of a second or third or fourth time back into that same hardship that was almost unbearable the last time through?

Humbled by how tenderly he has gathered broken pieces and shaped them into beauty and grace you could not have imagined?

Amazed by the evidence that God has been doing great things through you?

Throughout our lives, God takes us back and forth through these steps, perfecting, refining, renewing, rebuilding. Unlike the human potter, the Divine Potter is never finished but always bringing about something new. In us. And through us.

Now we have work to do.

Questions for Reflection and Discussion:

What step in the process do you most relate to in this season of your life?

Are there steps that you have been deliberately resisting, avoiding or neglecting? Ask God to make you willing to be made willing to surrender even to that process.

Prayer:

God, I am fearfully and wonderfully made. You called me into being and have shaped me by your hand. Through the circumstances of my life, times of long dryness, times of intense fire, times of immeasurable blessing, you have been at work in many, mighty ways. Thank you that I am your workmanship. Now, Lord, help me to be faithful to the work you are calling me to do, today and every day, and throughout all the seasons of my life. Here I am. Made by the master. Here I am. Ready for your use. Amen.

Recommended Reading

Bentz, Joseph. *When God Takes Too Long.* This book and the video that accompanies it give real help in understanding why things take so long, and what you can do to stay hopeful and productive in the meantime.

Foster, Richard. *Celebration of Discipline* and *Freedom of Simplicity.* There are several books that I make a point of re-reading regularly, and these are two that are especially meaningful for me. And humbling—I am always convicted and changed by what Foster has to say.

Keller, W. Phillip. *A Shepherd Looks at Psalm 23.* One of the most beautiful word pictures God gives us to describe himself is that of a shepherd watching over his sheep. Keller worked as a shepherd, and so when he reads the twenty-third Psalm, he understands the fullness of its meaning. A comforting, encouraging classic.

Lewis, C.S. *The Problem of Pain* and *A Grief Observed.* Sometimes we need help to understand why so many bad things happen and why God sometimes seems distant and unfair. Sometimes we need to know that other people have gone through times of personal hardship and know how we feel. Lewis has written both kinds of books: *The Problem of Pain* is an intellectual answer to the question of evil; *A Grief Observed* is the diary he kept when his wife, Joy Davidman, died. Each book is splendid in its own way.

Packer, J.I. *Knowing God.* A classic exploration of God's nature and character. Read it to get better acquainted with the God who loves you.

Sayers, Dorothy L. *The Mind of the Maker.* Sayers takes a thoughtful look at the nature of creativity and the ways in which God's creativity is reflected in us.

Willard, Dallas. *The Spirit of the Disciplines.* Substantial and thought-provoking, this book helps us understand how the spiritual disciplines become tools of transformation in our lives.

About the Author

Diana Pavlac Glyer is a potter, a painter, and an avid gardener. She teaches English at Azusa Pacific University. She enjoys the work of C.S. Lewis and J.R.R. Tolkien and has published books and articles about their creative process. She lives in southern California with her husband, Michael, and their beautiful daughter, Sierra Grace. For more information, visit her online at www.DianaGlyer.com

Clay in the Potter's Hands
was designed and composed by
The Seven-Seventy Design Group
in 11/16/22/42 Bookman Old Style
and published by
Lindale & Associates